POETRY
FOR THE *Soul*

POETRY
FOR THE *Soul*

Volume 2

Janice Stampley Means

iUniverse, Inc.
Bloomington

Poetry for the Soul
Volume 2

iUniverse books may be ordered through booksellers or by contacting:

iUniverse
1663 Liberty Drive
Bloomington, IN 47403
www.iuniverse.com
1-800-Authors (1-800-288-4677)

ISBN: 978-1-4759-6033-4 (sc)
ISBN: 978-1-4759-6034-1 (ebk)

Printed in the United States of America

iUniverse rev. date: 11/08/2012

POETRY FOR THE SOUL
Prose from the heart

DEDICATION

TO MY LOVING FAMILY
&
THE LATE HARDY & DOROTHY STAMPLEY

CONTENTS

"GREATER BLESSING"

I'm right where God wants me to be
In order to receive what he has for me
But I feel he has a greater blessing for my life
That's even more powerful than the gift to write
My writing is Gods' way of getting me exposed
And it's also for the cleansing of my soul
And he's using my writing to let people see
The powerful ministry he's placed in me
But there's a greater blessing on the way
And right now he's positioning me for that day

"ANOINTED"

I went through many trials because God knew
throughout my life
That I would minister words that would change
someone's life
I felt like I was going through living hell
But my anointing was so great he had to take me there
The people closest to me turned their backs and
treated me cruel
But the ones who hurt me most was who
God chose to use
I shed many tears behind people treating me wrong
But God said "Hold on I need my soldiers to be strong"
And once he delivered me and set me free
He birthed forth the gift that was inside of me
I endured many heartaches and was even abused
Before God said I was a vessel fit to be used
But he had to use extreme measures from the start

Because he knew I couldn't be use until he
humbled my heart
But now that I'm humble and under control
I've come too far to ever let go
And after all the pain and suffering
I endured in my life
I'm able to stand today as an anointed
woman in Christ

"LOOK AT ME"

Everyone I've talked to from my past
Is still talking about what they remember me doing last
But I want them to take a good look at me
And reflect on the person I've grown to be
Because once I got saved and changed my life
God said I was a new creature in Christ
So look at me now since I've changed my ways
And stop remembering me from the old days
Because all the things I did back then
Was the result of me living in a world of sin
But I've come a long way from the person I use to be
So take a look at me now and tell me what you see

"MY LOVER"*

I've passed many tests during my life
But still was convicted for not living right
Because after being blessed with the gift to write
I started sleeping with a man and wasn't his wife
And because I chose to sleep with my lover
God couldn't fully use me to minister to others
And since the bible says "You'll rather marry than burn"
I'm taking this as a lesson learned
But now I realize what I have to do
And that's make a decision between the two
Because God has a special love for me
That I'll never find between the sheets
So the only decision that I can see
Is either we depart or he marries me
Because I'll never receive that ultimate joy
If I just settle for being my lovers' toy
And since heaven is where I desire to dwell
I can't let having a lover send me to hell

"RACIAL IGNORANCE"

Racism is everywhere in this world today
But it's racial ignorance not to support your own race
Every race supports their own
But when it comes to mine you have to stand alone
Racial ignorance has held us down so long
And it's the same reason we can't get along
But if my race wasn't so jealous of one another
By standing together we could all go further
It seems like after all our ancestors went through
We'd support one another in whatever
we're trying to do
But instead we let our ignorance stand in the way
Of supporting an accomplishment that's made by our
own race
And we're quick to say we're not being treated right
But the real reason is we don't stand together and fight
That's why racial ignorance will always keep us down
But together our race can make a mighty sound

"STEP ASIDE"

I raised my children by myself
Only asking the system for a little help
And I always kept them both in church
Because it's important they do Gods' work
I raised them the best that I could
Like any good parent world
But I don't remember the exact day
They stopped listening to what I say
And started doing things I couldn't believe
To the point I wondered if they were my seed
Because as I was praising and glorifying Gods' name
My children was sinning like it was a game
But during that time God spoke to me
And he said "Beloved just let it be"
Since both your children are lost
You must stay faithful at all cost
Because you've done what I required you to do
And that was as a mother to raise the two
So just keep praying and step aside
And watch me work in both their lives

"SAME SPIRIT"

When I read the biography of Maya Angelou
I realized I possessed the same spirit too
Because we both have been blessed with the gift to write
To tell how we survived the trials in our life
And we both share our testimonies of how we survived
To help others deal with the adversities in their lives
And people acknowledge me just like Maya Angelou
As being a powerful influence in their lives too
And we share the same spirit in our hearts and minds
Because we both think the same although we're writing
from different times
And you can see the same spirit in the poems that we write
Because they reveal the hurt & pain we've endured all
our life

And we have a powerful way of expressing our words
To show the pain and triumph of heartbreak and love
And we're known to stand strong and speak loud and bold
When we're presenting a poem for the
people as a whole
But Maya Angelou has had the
honor to present
One of her poems at the inauguration of
the president
But I've written poems that I'm prepared to do
The day that I'm requested by the president too
And because we share the same spirit like we do
I may be blessed to be the next Maya Angelou

"THE PLAN"

It wasn't in Gods original plan
For women to be superior to man
Every woman upon this earth
Should truly know what she is worth
God gave women a rib from a man
But he gave us something extra if you can understand
God designed women to be unique
Haven't you ever wondered why Eve ate off the tree?
Eve proved to women that even back in the day
That they possessed a gift to make men do
things their way
So if we possess this power and know Gods plan
Then why are we being manipulated by man?
Women stepped out of the original plan
And started changing themselves trying to please a man
We try to keep men in all the wrong ways
By using children or material things to help along the way
We allow men to deprive us of our self-worth
And we compromise Gods word just to keep from
getting hurt

But all our endeavors have fallen in vain
Because nothing we've tried has stopped the pain
And as women if we don't take a stand
And get back in line with the original plan
Man will never see
Where God had predestined them to be

"SIGNS"

Things are no longer like they was in the past
Because God said one day the first will be last
And we can tell we're living in crucial times
Because every day we're seeing the signs
First we elected a black president
And now blacks are living in high class residents
And bills are being passed that will open doors
That'll take from the rich and give to the poor
But God didn't plan for anyone to be poor
But in fact he wanted us to have so much more
But people started getting the spirit of greed
And stopped helping others in their time of need
But don't lose your soul thinking money will
show your worth
Because the bible says one day "The last will be first"

"PLAYERS"

Most men consider themselves as players
But in reality they're only heart slayers
Because every woman that enters their life
Will only be a victim and never their wife
A players' main goal is to get your head
Just to see how fast he can get you in bed
And no matter how good you think you are
Making love isn't an option in a players' heart
That's why in bed they limit the things they do
Because they're not trying to fall in love with you
True players don't hold hands in the park
And they normally don't come around till after dark
So don't get the game twisted and think he loves you
Because you're just another number when he's
with his crew
And women are also considered players in this game
But when it comes to us we're just called a different name

"SUGAR COATED"

Gods given me a ministry that requires I bold
That's why I titled my books "Poetry for the Soul"
Because throughout my life I've always learned
To take this race serious that I have to run
Different struggles will come our way
That's especially designed to test our faith
That's why the words that's written in my poems
Are written in a way to help you reform
And they're not sugar coated to fit your needs
And lead you to destruction like the devil did Eve
Because when things are sugar coated they sound good
at the time
But can lead you to destruction down the line
And I'm a firm believer in what the bible says
And I won't mislead you in any way
That's why I gather the facts and state truth
So you can know exactly what you need to do
Because I want this gift that's been placed in me
To glorify God and set others free

"RECESSION"

There's something I want everyone to know
Don't gain the world and lose your soul
We all should have known in this day and time
That there would be a recession down the line
The bible warned us of plagues and wars
But we knew it would affect so much more
But God was preparing us for the day
That this thing called a recession would come our way
But if you're standing on his word you shouldn't be
having it hard
Because a recession don't affect the people of God
But if we look to the hills in which we get our help
We wouldn't worry about a recession or anything else

"COMING BACK"

For centuries we've heard people say
That God will be coming back one day
And the bible was left while he's away
To give us instructions along the way
But instead of reading and showing ourselves approved
We're going through life doing as we choose
And from lack of knowledge we're constantly
committing sin
And ignoring the fact he's coming back again
But if we read the bible we would see the signs
And would realize that we're running out of time
Because in the book of Revelation it specifically states
"That God will be coming back one day"

"STAND OUT"

I've always been able to stand out in a crowd
Some people say it's because I'm so loud
But I think God just wanted to show
That I have room in my life to grow
Because every opportunity given to me
He knew I was bold enough to receive
And now he's using how I used to be
To show the miraculous change in me
That's why I don't wonder or have any doubt
Why I was the one God chose to stand out

"LAST REQUEST"

My aunt received a call one night
And when the phone dropped I knew
something wasn't right
She told me my mother had been shot in the head
And immediately I assumed she was dead
But I didn't know she had time that day
To talk to my brother before she passed away
"Take care of your sisters was her last request
And then she closed her eyes and went into a
permanent rest
I remember the day after she died
Me and my sisters cried and cried
But my brother stood up like a man
Because he'd made a promise to do the best that he can
He still hadn't cried even after she was gone
But he knew we was hurting so he had to be strong
But late one night when he didn't think I knew
I saw him crying like a baby because he missed mama too
He did everything he possibly could
To take care of us like a big brother should
And even though he worked very late
He still brought food home to make sure we ate
But around this time things had gotten out of hand

Because one of his sisters' moved in with a man
And even though he didn't know what to do
He had a request he had to see through
And later while celebrating his birthday one night
He heard one of his sisters' had been cut in a fight
Someone had told him but he didn't have a clue
"Which sister? What happened? Or what should I do?"
But he took care of me until I got well
In hope I wouldn't retaliate and end up in jail
And by this time my brother was grown
And I really admired how he had held on
Eventually each of us graduated from school
And not only was we proud but our brother was too
Because if he hadn't stood by a promise he made
We wouldn't be the women we are today
And now God has blessed us to leave the nest
And we owe it to our big brother for fulfilling a last
request

"OUR CHILDREN"

We can tell we're in the last days
At the way our children have gone astray
They're walking around with bad attitudes
And armed with guns to do as they choose
They've stopped listening to what we say
And disrespecting their elders every day
But the bible told us we'd see the day
When our children would rebel in the worst way
And the time has come when we're seeing the signs
Of what to expect down the line
And all we can do as parents is pray
That their lunatic spirits will go away

"GOOD NEWS"

God is allowing me to spread the good news
About all the things that I've been through
And he wants me to let everyone know
How my testimonies have made me grow
That's why I'm sharing my good news with everyone
About all the grace I received from the Son
And how I was blessed with the gift to write
Showing how I came from darkness into his
marvelous light
Because every testimony that I've been through
Someone around the world is experiencing it too
That's why I can't keep this good news to myself
Because I want my testimonies to help someone else
And through the ministry god has given me to do
I've been given a chance to spread my good news

"NOBODY"

God has a reason for who he choose
And I'm just a vessel he decided to use
But to this world I'm just a nobody
That's trying to tell everybody about somebody
And since that somebody is our Savoir Jesus Christ
I'm hoping to inspire others to live right
And that's why he's using a nobody like me
To write and publish books about my testimonies
Because the people you think is a nobody to you
Are the very ones that God will choose to use

"TRY ME"

I don't know about you but there were times in my life
Where nothing I tried seemed to turn out right
My relationships never would last too long
And for the life of me I didn't know what was wrong
And every time I turned around
Something happened that would bring me down
But one day a friend said "when nothing else works
Sometimes the answer can be found at church"
But I didn't understand what she meant at the time
Because I'd tried everything that had crossed my mind
But one night during service I heard a minister say
There's a reason why things don't go the right way
He said "We cause ourselves a lot of pain and hurt
By trying everything else instead of putting God first
Because only God can change a situation over night
And give us that sense of peace we desire in our life"
So when you're ready to receive that eternal peace
God is simply saying "just try me"

"RUN & TELL"

I have no one but myself to blame
For how I've shamed my family name
I made decisions during my life
And it was my choice not to live right
But God allowed me a chance to change
So my testimonies wouldn't be in vain
And now I want people to run and tell
That God wants to use me instead of send me to hell
Because for a while the devil had me bound
And no family or friends wanted to be around
But all along God had it in his plan
That he'd do something that people wouldn't
understand
Because he wanted everyone to run and tell
That he conquered another soul that was bound for hell
People are quick to say what they see me doing wrong
But they want run and tell that I'm still standing strong
But now I can say that I'm no longer ashamed
Of how I'm carrying our family name

"USE TO BE"

No one under Gods eyes
Haven't done something they didn't want to hide
So don't think for a minute it's just you and me
Because everybody once was a use to be
During this walk there's one thing you'll see
People will always talk about what you use to be
I know I had a problem back in the day
But I gave it to Jesus and he took it away
And after being delivered I changed the things I do
So if he can forgive me then why can't you?
People come to Christ because they want to be free
They no longer want to be like they use to be
No one is perfect we're all the same
We've all done things that's shamed our name
When I was a gambler people talked about me

But now I'm delivered and God supplies all my needs
And since I'm not bound and has been set free
I don't worry when people talk about me
But what I do tell them is "yes that was me"
But I thank God that now I'm free
And then they'll say "That I haven't changed"
But look at where I am and from where I came
So it's alright for people to talk about you
Just make sure what they're saying isn't true
Because the devil has given them the words to say
To try to get you to return to your old ways
But as long as you stand strong, trust and believe
You'll never go back to what you use to be

"FALSELY ACCUSED"

I was talking to a man and I heard him say
How he had been falsely accused one day
And it made me wonder how women could be
So quick to lie about who conceived their seed
But when a woman wants her lifestyle to remain the same
The man with the most potential is who she'll blame
And if you're dealing with women that sleep with
different men
You should expect some hurt and confusion before it end
Because men have paid money and even served time
Just to find out the child not theirs down the line
And it makes them start carrying a lot of strife
And some turns on the children they raised all their life
Because their whole life changed when they were falsely
accused
And not only was he a victim but the children are too
And just like domestic violence this should also be a crime
Especially when it causes someone to have to serve time

"HEALED"

God you are a healer please me to heal
I know you didn't intend for me to hurt in your will
There are so many people hurting inside
Because they've been mistreated & constantly told lies
Please take this pain that I have in my heart
And show me how to forgive so the healing can start
Because there's so many things that I don't understand
Like why it hurts so bad when you get hurt from a man?
Whatever we do it's never enough
Because they'll still betray our love and trust
And we allow them to treat us any way they like
Even though how they're treating us just isn't right
There were many times I cried silent tears
Because it felt like I was losing my will to live
But the pain I'm feeling will never go away
If I keep holding on to yesterday
Please reach deep into my soul
And take away this pain that I hold
They say "what don't kill you can only make you strong
So is that why I've been hurting for so long?
But now that I've finally learned how to forgive
I thank God that now I'm healed

"NEVER SAID"

Ever since the day I got saved
I've experienced pure hell every step of the way
And even though God had paid the price
He never said I wouldn't have hardships in my life
But I always thought if I was living right
Things would get better in my life
But instead trials started coming every day
That was especially designed to test my faith
And then all of a sudden I began to see
My friends no longer came around me
And it seemed like the things I desired to do
Were the very things I didn't suppose too
But no one ever said it wouldn't be hard
Reforming from the world to living for God
But even though it hasn't been easy
I know he didn't bring me this far to leave me

"CHANGE"

Before I ever start dating a man
There's something about me he must understand
My parents have already raised me
Into the woman I need to be
And he'll have to accept the things I say
Because my sense of humor won't go away
And even if I met Mr. Right
He couldn't even make me change my life
Because I've been independent for a long time
And God has given me a peace of mind
And since I was designed from Gods' perfect plan
I'll never change to please a man

"CHEATERS"

People that cheat have a spirit of lust
And don't realize they're betraying someone's trust
They don't stop and think about anyone else
Because they're only focus is on their self
And they don't care that they're breaking your heart
Because if they did they wouldn't cheat from the start
And a guilty conscious is always your proof
Because they'll take the blame off them and start
accusing you
And because you're hurt you'll constantly call their phone
Or drive by their house to see if they're home
And then you'll get upset because you don't have a clue
On what you've done to make them cheat on you
And even though you know it's probably just sex
It still hurts to know they're with someone else
But the bad thing about cheaters is they never know
How someone will handle letting them go
Because some people may break down and cry
But some go as far as committing suicide
God said a liar can't tally his sight
And a cheater has to lie every day and night
So if you know God sees all that you do
Don't let the label cheater be placed on you

"I LOVE YOU"

Whenever I'm talking to my family or friends
I always say "I love you" before the conversation ends
Because you never know what's on a person's mind
Even though they're saying that everything's fine
So don't hang up the phone too fast
Because that conversation may be your last
And "I love you" is something that everyone should hear
Every now and then coming through their ears
The bible says love will conquer all
And I'd rather show you love than to see you fall
And since God shows love in all that he do
It shouldn't be hard to say "I love you"

"A CRIME"

My son committed a serious crime
And ended up having to do some time
But it isn't as bad as it may seem
Because while he was there he was redeemed
At first he use to cry every day
Not knowing that God would make way
But God will forgive us for whatever we do
As long as we come to him in spirit and truth
And by him knowing the wages of sin is hell
He cried out to Jesus from the bed of his cell
And then God used his remaining time there
To show him that he still cared
Because the system was meant to bring him down
But God turned his situation around
And now the visits are no longer the same
All because a crime made him call on Jesus name

"PACKAGE DEAL"

I'm trying my best to stay in Gods' will
But it's vital that I have the package deal
Because if I'm going to make it in this world of sin
I'll need the package deal in order to win
My father is the one who gave me life
But the Son is the one who paid the price
And the Holy Spirit is oh so real
That's why I must have the package deal
Because together they all play a major role
In determining the salvation of my soul
And as long as I'm covered by the package deal
Nothing can take me out of Gods' will

"SACRIFICE"

God said to "sacrifice for someone else
And take the focus off yourself"
But my children don't know what I've been through
Trying to take care of them and myself too
I've had to make sacrifices every day
Regardless of what they think or say
I've sacrificed by doing things I knew was wrong
Just so they could have a good home
And I've went as far as to deny Gods' will
And shacked up with men just to pay the bills
I've sacrificed myself in so many ways
And I'm still sacrificing to this day
But one of these days I hope they'll see
That I've sacrificed my whole life for them and not me

"MY COMFORTER"

Very few people could walk in my shoes
And go through the things that I have too
Because after being blessed with the gift to write
All hell broke loose in my life
I had to live without power and even food
Not knowing from day to day what I was going to do
And I lost my job for no reason at all
And it resulted in me getting my car turned off
But what the devil did for evil God used it for good
And sent me a comforter like he said he would
And he made it so visible for me to see
That all along my faith was the key
And he opened up for me so many doors
So I could receive everything I lost and more
And now during an attack I just stay strong in my faith
Because I know that my comforter is on the way

"A MAMAS BOY"

Ever since my youngest son was born
He's been stuck to me just like a thorn
But now that he's away from home
I know he's feeling all alone
Because there hasn't been a day go by
That he wasn't right there by my side
And even now that he's grown
He still don't sleep till I come home
He's a mamas' boy to his heart
And he's been that way from the very start
And it hurts for me to know that he's gone
But it's time this mamas' boy stand on his own

"BEING MYSELF"

People always tell me that during this walk
There's a correct way that I need to talk
So I watched talk shows to see what they say
In hope I could learn to speak the correct way
But when all failed I went to God for help
And he said "Beloved just be yourself
Because you're the one who endured the pain
That you received for my name
And the way you talk is how people will see
What made you the woman you've grown to be"
So I stopped trying to change the way I talk
Because it's part of my testimony during this walk
And that's why God said to be myself
Because I can tell my testimonies better than anyone else

"TRANSFORMATION"

Transformation is a process I had to undergo
It was needed for my thinking but mainly for my soul
Because it says in Romans chapter 12
"Be not conformed to this world"
One night while getting ready for the club
I was blessed to receive a sign from above
And since I was tired of not living right
Instead of going to the club I went to church that night
And before the service ended I received a word
And my transformation began off of what I heard
But first I had to be ready to change my life
From a lifetime of sin to living for Christ
But my transformation still couldn't fully start
Until after I allowed God to humble my heart
And it made me see things in a different way
To the point I changed everything I did and say

"ME"

Not only does my poetry set others free
But it's also very inspirational to me
Because it's my way of letting go
The pain I've held deep in my soul
And I don't want people to misunderstand
So I refer to the bible as much as I can
Because Gods' word will never change
And my poetry is written to glorify his name
So before ministering to you I first minister to myself
Because I need it as much as anyone else
So as you read my poetry I hope you can see
It's not just helping you but it's also helping me

"WORLD OF SIN"

We often find ourselves in a world of sin
And want to get out but don't know where to begin
Because right when we think we've gotten on track
Something happens that pulls us back
And we try to figure out what we can do
That could possibly help us make it through
But it seems like whatever we attempt to try
Just pulls us closer by the wayside
But if we wait for the help that only God can send
It'll keep us out of a world of sin

"GOD IS GOOD"

I've started doing things I never thought I would
And all I can say is God is good
He's made a dramatic change in my life
By taking me to higher heights
And he's opened doors that's been shut in my face
From people that judged me because of my race
But people from everywhere will soon see
The powerful gift God has placed in me
And if he did it for me he'll do it for you
Because God is good in all that he do

"HELP ME"

Lord please help me "what am I doing wrong?"
I've endured many trials so I know that I'm strong
I'm trying my best to live the right way
But different struggles are coming each day
Please help me use what you've placed in me
Because there's so much that the world needs to see
You're on my mind every day and night
And that's how I get my motivation to write
At first I was thinking I was writing about me
But it was to help others in their time of need
The enemy wants me sidetracked and confused
But help me keep my focus only on you
He's trying to use my children to stand in the way
Of what you want me to do and say
Please help me keep the love in my heart
That you placed in me from the very start
Because I want my writing to help someone
This isn't something I'm doing for fun
So help me Lord you're the only one who knows
How to help my inner ministry grow

"YOUR CHILD FIRST"

Lord only you could know
How it feels for me to let my child go
I've sheltered him until he was grown
And now I need the strength to stay strong
My insides feel empty and hurt
But I have to remember he was your child first
Just knowing I carried him and gave him birth
Only makes the pain feel worst
And whenever I see my child cry
It makes me feel like I want to die
Please help me Lord to understand
He's no longer my baby but a man
But he's made a mistake that's changed his life
And being mad at the world won't make it right
But I know that he will make it through
His faith is being tested and mine is too
So shed grace on the child that I gave birth
And help me remember he was your Child first

"MY SON'S"

I brought into the world two little boys
And they've been my pride and joy
I raised them the best that I could
Just like any good mother would
They both are charming in their own way
And they always keep a smile on their face
And if you look into their eyes
You'll see their sentimental side
I'll always be there when they need me to be
Because my son's mean the world to me
And I'll never let anything or anyone
Come between me and my son's

"INTERFERE"

By law my son has become a man
But spiritually there's things he don't understand
I promised God when he comes home next year
That I'll no longer interfere
Because regardless if he choose to do wrong or right
I can't change the plan that God has for his life
There will be times he'll need some advice
But unfortunately I can't tell him how to live his life
All I can hope is that he understands
That his destiny lies in Gods' hands
But by not interfering doesn't mean I can't pray
That he'll make the right decisions along the way

"A LIVING TESTIMONY"

"MY MARKS"

In Galatians chapter 6 verse 17
Shows that God resides inside of me
And because he used a filthy vessel like me
It may cause people not to receive
But as long as I carry on my body these marks
I refuse to let anyone trouble my heart
And even when they laugh or talk behind my back
I don't worry because God will handle all that
Because if God is for me in all that I do
I can't be trying to please man too
Because God is using me to minister to his sheep
And whatever I sow I shall also reap
And I can't get weary in doing Gods' work
That's why I praise him constantly at home and in
church
And these marks I've carried throughout my life
Should prove I bare the spirit of our Savoir Jesus Christ

"LIFE & DEATH"

Someone please call 911
But don't send an officer I need Jesus to come
There's a life and death situation at hand
Because the enemy has gotten into the minds of man
And he telling them all sorts of lies about you
And because they don't know you they're believing it's true
So I pray a minor miracle be sent my way
So I'll know what to write and what to say
But I have to be careful about what I say
Because I can't afford to push them away
Because every minute that I let go by
Someone is falling by the wayside
We don't need to put these people in jail
Because they're already bound for hell
But they have a life and death urgency need
That's why it's vital that I get them to believe
And they need to realize their salvation is at stake
And it's important that they finish this race
So I need the Holy Spirit, the Father and the Son
To get them to change before the rapture comes

"CELL PHONE"

Cell phones are very popular today
But what if we treated the bible the same way
Would it be distributed all over the world
To every man, woman, boy and girl?
And would it always be carried around
And opened up when there's something to be found?
And would we feel lost all day long
If we made a mistake and left it at home?
I don't know about you
But my cell phone can't do what the bible can do
A cell phone is designed for on the go
But the bible is equipped to save my soul
And a cell phone can break at any time
And cause confusion instead of peace of mind
But the bible is given as a guide to live
And with a cell phone you'll only get a bill

"STRAYING AWAY"

I never thought after I got saved
That one day I would stray away
Because after God took away the pain
Nothing in my life was ever the same
I started receiving blessings all the time
But most of all I gained a peace of mind
But then one day my family was attacked
And I took my focus off God and started looking back
And before I knew what had happened to me
I started having doubts in what I believe
And begin doing things I'd done in the past
Forgetting what only God has for me will last
But now I'm back seeking God every day
And asking for forgiveness for straying away

"BULLYING"

I pray for the parents who've experienced pain
Behind their children's lives being taken in vain
And I'm also praying for the parents who
Have become victims behind things their children do
Because the parents can't apologize and make it right
After their child cause someone to take their own life
But I do blame the government for taking God out of
schools
Because that's when bullying because widespread on
the news
But since bullying has been going on for so long
People don't look at it as something wrong
But bullying will only get worst down the line
If we keep on neglecting to see the signs
Because if people continue to treat others cruel
Death is the result of what bullying can do
But in our hearts we know bullying isn't right
Especially if it causes someone to take their own life

"WON'T COMPLAIN"

I've complained most of my adult life
About things I thought wasn't turning out right
But I no longer will complain
Because my testimonies aren't falling in vain
And since God has opened up so many doors
I vowed to not complain anymore
Because complaining only allowed God to see
I didn't trust the plan he had for me
And now that I'm living in his marvelous light
I won't complain about the plan he has for my life

"POETRY"

My poetry is written in a unique way
Because it relates the message that I'm trying to say
Because at one point I didn't have a clue
On exactly what God wanted me to do
But then I was blessed with a gift so rare
That I could use anywhere
But my poetry not only tells about my life
It's also to inspire others to live right
And it gives me a great sense of pride
Knowing my heavenly father is by my side
And my poetry has made it possible for me
To help others in their time of need

"NEVER QUESTION"

My mother use to always say
Never question God in anyway
Because he's with us throughout our life
Whether we're living wrong or right
And all we have to do is trust
That God knows what's best for us
And we shouldn't question what he puts us through
Because there's a reason for everything he do
And since God created everything on this earth
No one should ever question his work

"POOR REPRESENTATION"

My son was sentenced and sent away
After being poorly represented one day
Because if his case had been presented right
It wouldn't have caused him 3 yrs. of his life
But I didn't have any money at the time
To get a paid attorney for down the line
And I know the decision that was made won't change
But it still was a cause for me to campaign
Because I felt the need to take a stand
And speak out on the issues at hand
because even though the judge decides what to do
Poor representation caused my son to lose
And by speaking about his representation that day
Hopefully will cause others to take a stand the same way

"ATTACKED"

A storm came and my family was attacked
And we went from living comfortable to experiencing lack
I had been out of work about a month or two
So when my son's got in trouble I didn't know what to do
But by me being in church and already saved
I knew that God would make a way
But the attacks started coming more and more
I even experienced the law kicking in my door
And while the attacks was a their worst
I made a bad decision and stopped going to church
But when attacks start turning into devastating blows
Church is the best place that you can go
Because that's where you'll find that prayer is the only way
To withstand the attacks that'll come each day

"HOLD ME DOWN"

My family and friends just don't know
How over the years they've hurt me so
When I thought they should be there for me
They turned their backs in my time of need
I feel like they're trying to hold me down
By not supporting me or coming around
I know I shouldn't be feeling this way
Because God is behind what I write and say
But I refuse to let anyone hold me down
From spreading Gods' word all over town
He's the author but I did the work
And no one will hold me down from spreading the gift
that I gave birth

"NO OBLIGATION"

There are lots of women on the prowl
Seeking married men whom they can devour
Once she sees he's wearing a ring
Shortly after she'll start to scheme
And after getting his attention she'll do and say
Things to him in a flirty way
She'll give him her number and tell him its fine
For him to call when he has time
And eventually he'll call to see if she's home
And to make sure that she's all alone
And later he'll start mistreating his wife
So he can have a reason to leave home at night
But one day he asked her "where have she been"
And she said "why? We're nothing but friends"
Because all along she had it in her plans
To eventually drop him and find another man
But the signs were there for him to see
That she only wanted a man that wasn't free
And the bible says "submit only to your wife"
And now he realizes what messed up his life
He allowed his self to fall under temptation
By submitting to a women with no obligation

"DEATH"

What is it about death that scares people so?
Just like we come to this world one day we'll have to go
And death is nothing but a permanent sleep
So why do people mourn and weep?
God allowed death to take his own seed
And his blood was the price for you and me
Because he wanted God to give us another chance
To redeem ourselves upon this land
But there's a day and time we all must go
And when death comes only God will know
And since death has no appointed time
We want God to be pleased at what he'll find
God said he comes like a thief in the night
But death shouldn't scare you if you're living right
So prepare yourself as you run this race
Because death has no appointed time nor place

"AS ONE"

Every time someone's marriage breaks down
Their business is spread all over town
You'll start hearing something everyday
Because people just have to have something to say
But there's one thing that they don't see
If you're talking about him you're talking about me
And even if he's out there running the streets
If something happens to him it'll also affect me
That's why I hate for someone to tell me what he do
Even though I know some of it may not be true
But the feelings I have in my heart won't change
Because he's still the one who gave me his last name
And it hurts to know that we're apart
Because he holds the other half of my heart
But regardless of what he may have done
As long as we're married we'll always be as one

"VISUAL"

God put in my visual what you want me to see
And give me a visual of who you want me to be
I know you want me to live the right way
And I'm striving to do your will everyday
But Jesus you're the only one who knows
How to direct my path on which way to go
Because this world I'm living in is full of sin
But I'm determined to be victorious in the end
So put in my visual the things I can do
To send out the messages you want me too

"BREAK UPS"

People can be together for years at a time
And then experience a break up down the line
And even though their feelings are no longer the same
Doesn't mean their hearts have changed
Because every time a relationship ends
Someone will eventually start dating again
And you'll think they no longer care about you
Because of all the things you see them do
But if the truth be told they care more than you know
That's just how they're dealing with letting you go
Because during a break up people tend to do
Whatever it takes to get their mind off of you
And even though someone has taken your place
There are some things the heart won't let the mind erase
Like all the times you shared in the past
Not knowing that the relationship wouldn't last
But break ups are something that's hard to do
So don't think that it's easy for either of you

"MY MOTHER"

My mother touched people in so many ways
Because she did something special everyday
If someone had a problem in the neighborhood
My mother would be the first to help if she could
And even though she had six children of her own
She adopted three more because they didn't have a home
And she did things for the children in the neighborhood
That none of the other parents would
Like taking all the children to the Natchez Trace
So we could play kickball and sometimes race
But most of all she kept us all in church
Because she was a firm believer of doing Gods' work
It's easy to know my mother by just knowing me
Because the apple don't fall to far from the tree

"TALK"

For the life of me I just can't see
What gives someone the right to talk about me
I'm trying my best to live the right way
But they still talk about me anyway
But the bible says that during this walk
I can't control the way that people talk
But I feel like it's a crying shame
At the length someone would go to shame my name
That's why every night when I'm on my knees
I pray for the one's that talk about me

"LETTING GO"

Everyone knows that it's hard to be friends
Whenever a relationship comes to an end
And I was taught you have to love yourself
Before you can love anyone else
But people will go from day to day
Walking around with their hearts in pain
But their hearts wouldn't hurt so bad inside
If they could forget their foolish pride
But you think about how you use to be adored
And now that person don't want you anymore
And it hurts to know you've grown apart
Because the love you once shared is still in your heart
And even though he treated you wrong
It's still hard to leave him alone
But life is too short for us to not see
That some things just aren't meant to be
But over the years as you grow
You'll know when it's time for you to let go

"NICKNAME"

Most people are given nicknames as a child
And it seems alright for a little while
But there comes a time as you grow
Your nickname won't serve the same purpose anymore
Because when living in the world you do things a
certain way
And your nickname is associated with what you do and say
And most people will learn your nickname very fast
Because it's easier for them to attach it to your past
But God said when a person has changed their life
They then become a new creature in Christ
And that's why your nickname can't remain the same
Because everything in your life including your name
must change
And as you begin your journey in living for Christ
Don't let your nickname be attached to your life

"MISCARRIAGES"

I've experienced heartaches from miscarriages during
my life
But it wasn't a medical reason it was from not being
treated right
And I always wondered if they'd made it to this world
Would they have been a boy or a girl
My miscarriage wasn't caused because of my health
They were caused by the hands of someone else
And by me knowing my babies was already formed
Made me blame myself that they were never born
Because if I hadn't allowed myself to keep be physically
abused
I wouldn't have had one miscarriage lest known two
But by me allowing a man to fight me all the time
Deprived my babies of life down the line
But I'm happy to know that they aren't alone
Because during the miscarriage God took them back home
No one knows the pain I've carried throughout my life
Just knowing I allowed a man to take my child's life

"A CLIQUE"

In my past I was wild and loud
But I never was the one to hang with a crowd
And I never did things that other people do
Because I was the type to make my own rules
And being in a clique was never my cup of tea
Because can't nobody tell me what to believe
Because when someone in a clique is mad at you
All their friends have to be mad too
So don't let being in a clique steer you wrong
That's why God gives you a mind of your own

"THE RACE"

During church one Sunday they were singing a song
That said "I wrestled with the angels all night long"
And it seemed like the pastor was talking to me
When he asked "Are you where God wants you to be"
But it's hard for a person to start living right
After living in sin all their life
Because there were times I repented every day
Just for minor sins I committed along the way
And it had nothing to do with listening to the word
Or applying to my life what I had heard
Because I'm a believer and I pray everyday
But I'll still backslide despite Gods' grace
And every since I proclaimed to be saved
The devil has attacked me every step of the way
And even though I'm vessel that God chose to use
You have to remember I'm still in the flesh
And every day the devil travels to and fro
Trying his best to conquer my soul
So no matter how hard I strive to live right
I'll always have temptation in my life
But as for me, if the truth be told
I think I'm doing good by just not letting go
Because this race isn't easy that we have to run
That's why God had to sacrifice his only begotten son

"CHARGED"

While I was having surgery my sons was left alone
And I had no clue what was happening in my home
But after coming home the law kicked in my door
And immediately I was handcuffed on the floor
I wasn't worried because I'd done nothing wrong
But they charged me because I was the only one at home
But I can't understand being charged with a crime
When I was in the hospital during that time
But they used the law as an excuse
To justify what they wanted to do
But I thank God I wasn't arrested that day
And only received a ticket to pay
And even though they falsely charged me that day
I knew God was covering me every step of the way

"FAMILIES TESTIMONIES"

Give me a moment to testify
How God stopped death from talking our lives
Once I was brutally cut in a fight
But God didn't let me die that night
And my sister was sick for awhile
Because she had cancer as a child
And one sister had MS and lost control
But didn't get killed on the road
And my brother was almost shot one day
Because his spouse was feeling betrayed
And I know it wasn't in Gods' will
For both my sister and mother to be killed
And he also didn't have it in his plan
For my sister to die from the hands of a man
And my brother don't use any medications today
Because God took his asthma away
And all the testimonies you've heard today
Came from God shedding his mercy and grace

"RUNNING"

We all experience relationships that don't turn out right
But I've been in one that had me running for my life
I was with a man that didn't want to let go
Who was killing my spirit and aiming for my soul
His addiction caused him to abuse me all the time
To the point I almost lost my mind
And when I tried to leave and go on with my life
He would always find me and start a fight
But when I realized he'd never treat me right
I took my kids and started running for my life

"BAD RELATIONSHIPS"

After being in bad relationships all my life
I'm finally in one that turned out right
He knows what happened in my past
That caused my relationships not to last
And by knowing this it gave him a clue
On what he should and should not do
And I know he has my best interest at hand
Because he tries to please me anyway he can
But the reason I know our relationship will work
Is because we both chose to put God first

"JADA BABY"

When Jada was born she was a sheer delight
And I would keep her morning, noon and night
I use to lay her on a blanket on my bed
And sit and rub her little bald head
And every time she came to stay with me
I'd lay her on my stomach just to put her to sleep
She was the prettiest little girl I'd ever seen
But I wasn't shocked because she had my family genes
And as she grew she started walking on her toes
Like her head was leading her everywhere she go
She made these funny faces & acted a certain way
That's why I started calling Flossy Mae
I noticed she did whatever she saw me do
Because when I praised God she praised him too
And I thank God I'm able to see her grow
Because she's my 1st grandchild and I love her so

"THE JUDICIAL SYSTEM"

The judicial system is no better today
It's just set up in a different way
Because once the constitution was signed
It should have abolished racism down the line
But the system found another way
To legalize what they do and say
Because I was a victim of a black on black crime
And my assailant didn't have to serve a day of time
But a lesser crime changed my child's life
But in his case the victim was white
And everyone knows it was no mistake
How gallons of oil entered our rivers and lakes
But they knew if it didn't get stopped in time
It would fall on the president down the line
But that's just another one of their ways
In trying to take the presidents seat away
But together we can take a stand
And change the judicial system in our land

"JUDGED"

When I was a child I had a hard life
And the last thing on my mind was trying to live right
I was a child in age but living like I was grown
But I needed to survive so I had to be strong
Every morning my day would begin
By waking up and taking a sip of gin
But before you judge me let me tell you why
I was only a child and it was after my mother died
And since I could do whatever I wanted too
I would club all night and then go to school
I had gotten caught up in a world of sin
So I lived like the world was coming to an end
I lied, stole and cheated even though it was wrong
But no one gave me anything so I got it on my own
But there was a purpose for me in Gods' will
That down the line I would have to fulfill
So what the devil meant for evil God used it for good
That's why I turned out differently than everyone
thought I would
And the way that people judged back in the day
Is what made me the woman I am today

"TO A LOVED ONE"

I felt like this is the right time
To tell you what's been on my mind
I never found the time to talk to you
About all the things you've put me through
So this is my only way
To get you to listen to what I have to say
The day you decided to make me your wife
Was probably the happiest day of my life
But I hoped and prayed that you would change
After choosing to give me your last night
I never dishonored the vows I made
And I'm still honoring them to this day
But you insisted on cheating knowing it was wrong
Not caring that it was affecting our home
And you asked for forgiveness time after time
Knowing you'd cheat again down the line
I should have stopped it from the start
But I stood by and allowed you to break my heart
But I'll never let you put me through this again
Even if it causes our marriage to end
So I hope you're serious about making a new start
Because what I'm saying is coming straight from the heart

"A PICTURE"

While looking in the paper I saw a familiar face
And I wondered what happened that made him stray away
Unfortunately it was a picture of my youngest son
And I was still devastated at what he had done
He was the type of child that always went to work
And every Sunday he went with me to church
But he started hanging out with the wrong friends
And gave the devil enough room to step in
And even though he's locked up at the age of 18
God is still working behind the scene
And I don't believe a picture can determine his fate
Because God knows his heart and it's not too late

"BOLDNESS"

People use to say that loud and bold
And always did the opposite of what I was told
It didn't take anything for me to speak my mind
And would be ready to fight at the drop of a dime
And I had a reputation over town
To always start drama when I came around
But the same boldness that I had back then
Is what God wants to use in the messages that I send
That's why when he changed me and set me free
He left that same boldness inside of me
Because he knew that there would come a time
That I could use that boldness down the line

"IDOLS"

We can make our life easy or we can make it hard
But we'll soon realize that we have a jealous God
And his 1st commandments specifically reads
"Worship no image or idol before me
And even though I thought I was living right
I was worshipping idols I obtained during my life
But because of my ignorance I didn't understand
That an idol can be material as well as man
And one day I heard my pastor say
"That God can give it and he can take it away"
But I didn't see it until the day
Both my job and license was taken away
Because my great paying job was what I used
To obtain my beautiful house and my cars too
But eventually things started getting bad
And I ended up losing everything I had
But God took everything because I didn't receive
His 1st commandment "Worship No Idol before Me"

"LUVIN"

No matter what I went through during my life
My puppy was with me morning, noon and night
most people say a dog is a man's best friend
But to a woman going through a dog can be a godsend
There were many nights I laid in bed and cried
And Luvin would come lay by my side
And when I was bored and had nothing to do
She would chase my hands to keep me amused
Even though she was a dog she acted like a child
And she kept me busy during my trials
I never had a moment to focus on my pain
Because when I needed a friend I just called her name
She always jumped and growled at anyone
That she felt was close enough to do me some harm
Protecting me was her way of showing she cared
And that's why I call her "mama" because she's always
there
God sent Luvin as a companion to me
Because he knew she'd love me unconditionally

"SEPERATIONS"

A separation is the beginning of the middle and the end
It's a partnership that didn't suppose to end
It's a painful experience when two hearts are torn apart
Because everything plays a part in the matters of the heart
The bible says "you can separate for a season"
But it doesn't say for any reason
A separation can cause a lot of heartache and pain
Because the way you use to live will never be the same
When you got married they promised a lifetime of devotion
But instead all they did was play with your emotions
And now it's come down to one of the two
Either you leave me or I'll leave you
And even though you said you wanted them gone
You still wonder what in the world went wrong
And after a while the loneliness sets in
And it makes you feel like you've lost your best friend
And then one day they'll be coming your way
And you'll go another direction because you don't know
what to say

And even though you're missing them with all your heart
The devils' job is to keep you apart
Because he knows as long as he keeps you apart
You'll eventually lose the love you still have in your heart
But if time goes by and you see you still care
You should rekindle the love that you once shared
Because even though you had your reasons for letting
them go
A separation is for a season to give your heart time to grow

"HIGHER"

Lord since I've been living right
You've taken me to higher heights
And there's so much that I can see
I can do with this gift you've given me
And by you opening up so many doors
Give me a chance to glorify you more
Because the higher I'm elevated in this walk
The more people I can stand before and talk
And I know everyone around me can see
That talking about you is exciting to me
And I have a boldness like never before
To do your will more and more
And as I'm taken to a higher place
I'll glorify you every step of the way

"MISTREATED"

My sons would rather I be alone
Than to bring a man into our home
Because they don't have any say
When I'm not being treated the right way
There were times they'd see me cry
And would come to my room and sit by my side
And when they say "they love me" I know it's true
And I tell them that I love them too
But now both my sons are grown
And they're still watching who I bring home
Because they're tired of seeing me hurt
From being in relationships that just don't work
So if a man's not God filled and living right
My sons won't allow him to be in my life

"RELEASE"

God showed me how to release my pain
And it's made my life forever change
Because I found out a long time ago
Before you can move on you have to let go
And now that he's given me the gift to write
I can release the hurt I've held all my life
And I can also help others by letting them know
How they too can release what's in their soul
Because sometimes the pain and anger is so deep
That it can cause you to lose sleep
But by releasing what you have on your mind
Can help you move on down the line

"MY CHILDREN"

My children think I don't hear what they say
But I take time to listen to them everyday
Because everything they say or do
Not only affect them but it affects me too
That's why I tell them to watch what they say
Because their words could catch up with them one day
And I try not to interfere in their life
Unless I see them making the same mistake twice
And I always keep up with where they go
So if something happens I'll be the first to know
But whenever the time comes and they decide to leave
They can always come to me in their time of need

"THE NEWS"

There's so much happening on the news
From the result of killings, robberies and abuse
And the courts is only giving them time
After they've committed these hideous crimes
But the reason that people are acting this way
Is because Gods' been taken out of everything today
And once God was taken out of schools
Children started bullying, talking back and being rude
And they can't be chastised for what they do
Because now parents can be charged with abuse
But chastisement is a form of love
And that comes from the man above
And as a society there are things we can do
To force the government to put God back in schools
Because I'm a witness the day will come
When you'll be watching the news and see your
daughter or son

"WATCHED"

By me being single made it hard to live right
So I felt that it was time for me to change my life
Because my sons watched everything that I did
And it made it hard to keep something hid
Because whenever my boyfriend and I would fight
They were always concerned if I was alright
And I reassured them that I would be fine
And this wouldn't keep happening down the line
But not only are they watching me but God is too
And he promised to cover me in whatever I go through

"A GAMBLER"

We all receive habits from our father or mother
And one will always be worse than the other
But how could it be out of all my sisters and brothers
That I'm the only one that gambled like my mother
It all started when I was young
I use to watch her gamble and it looked like fun
And I kept the thought in back of my mind
Never thinking I'd be addicted down the line
But during my life I begin finding ways
To go somewhere and gamble everyday
But one day my father was on the phone
And he said "you need to leave that gambling alone
Because I never seen it in your sisters and brothers
But you've become a gambler just like your mother"
And then I started praying about it everyday
And by the grace of God he took it away

"HIT"

I brought two boys into this world
And taught them never to hit a girl
Because God created women to be a helpmate
Not to be abused by being hit or shacked
If God intended for women to be hit by a man
He would've created them with a bat in their hands
But if you've allowed a man to hit you at any time
You can expect him to do it again down the line
Because some men don't see it as a disgrace
To go around hitting women in their face
But every man that's upon this earth
Should remember it was a woman who gave them birth

"STRUGGLES"

All the struggles I've encountered each day
Came because I wasn't living the right way
My struggles began after my mother passed
And also because I was living too fast
But over time I begin to see
That God was spreading his grace on me
And because I was tired of living the wrong way
I started going to church and eventually got saved
And when God saw I was changing my life
He brought me out of darkness and into his
marvelous light
And now my struggles have become less and less
Because I realize now they're just a series of tests
And even though I'm still struggling I'm in a position to
receive
Everything that God has for me

"CRAZY FAITH"

As a believer it's required of me
To have the faith of a mustard seed
And I have the kind of faith that when I pray
I'll see a manifestation right away
Because whenever I'm blessed to hear Gods' word
Something touches my spirit from above
And when I'm promised a breakthrough will come
My crazy faith makes me get up and run
And I don't care who's watching me
Because I know who God has called me to be
And since faith is things hoped for but not yet seen
I want everything that's been promised to me
So when you see me running and giving God praise
It's just my crazy faith that has me acting that way

"WRONG CHURCH"

I was speaking with a friend and it dawned on me
Are we in the church we supposed to be?
Because sometimes we're blind and it's hard to see
That if you're in the wrong church you can't receive
And if you're in the wrong church you will know
Because you'll never see yourself spiritually grow
And you'll never be able to conquer your sins
Because you're leaving as empty as you came in
And when people are in need of urgent help
They turn to the church before anyone else
And when the church won't help in their time of need
They wonder if they're where they suppose to be
Because church is where they expect the kind of love
Like that which comes from our Savior above
But Gods' people are falling by the wayside
Because churches are focusing mainly on their tithes
But things must be in order for God to prevail
And being in the wrong Church can send you to hell

"POSITIVE"

I want my life to reflect what I say
That's why I write my poems in a positive way
Because through my writing I'm planting a seed
In hope to help others in their time of need
And I want my books to inspire someone's life
And hopefully motivate them to live right
And since many people will read them down the line
I must speak positive at all times
Because through the messages that I'm trying to send
I have to speak positive to be victorious in the end

"LOST"

I was talking to someone on the phone one day
And realized he was lost when I heard him say
"People will always have it hard
Going through life believing there's a God"
And I tried to tell him "be careful what you say
Because God is watching us every day"
And by him being lost and his spirit being dead
I tried reciting a verse that I had read
But he said "he didn't care about what I heard
Because he's never believed in Gods' word"
And then he told me to "leave him alone"
So I respected his wishes and hung up the phone
But I couldn't believe someone could be so lost
To have sold their soul at all cost
So I got down on my knees and prayed
For God to help him find his way

"THE BLOOD"

I saw while reading the Gospel of John
That we have eternal life through the blood of the Son
His blood was shed on Calvary for me
From the nails in his hands to the holes in his feet
And he stopped the world from coming to an end
By shedding his blood for the remission of our sins
And through Jesus we're given a chance to change
So our testimonies won't be in vain
And if we plead the blood while we're going through
There's nothing that the devil can do
Because Jesus gave his son out of love
And that's why all power lies in the blood
So plead the blood every day and night
Over both you and your family's life

"VALUES"

Unfortunately my mother has passed and gone
But she left her values to carry on
She gave me everything that I need
To grow into the woman I needed to be
But the best value she installed in me
Were the ones that could help set me free
Like living for God and going to church
And sowing seeds to show my worth
And now that I'm finally grown
My values is what's keeping me strong
And the same values she installed in me
Are the same one's I want to install in my seed

"MY SPIRIT"

One day I spoke with one of my friends
And was shocked to find out she had given up on men
She told me her life now belonged to Christ
And every day she was striving to live right
I asked her "what did she do after work"
And she said " go to functions with her church"
She said "it's been years since she's been with a man
Because they don't want to comply with Gods plan"
And she's standing firm on what she wants to do
Because she knows that God will see her through
My spirit revealed to me after we walked
That she'd be victorious during this walk

"KNOWLEDGE"

I was always told as a young girl
That knowledge is the most powerful things in this world
And that's why I read and show myself approved
So I can live the way God require me too
The bible tells us that in the last days
That false Prophets will come our way
But if I read and have knowledge of my own
No one would be able to steer me wrong
Because knowledge not only helps me live right
But it helps in every aspect of my life
That's why knowledge is the most powerful tool
That God left behind for us to use

"RESPONSIBILITY"

I raised two sons and a younger brother
And even though he wasn't mine I still was like his
mother
There was nothing I would do for J.D & POO
That I wouldn't do for my Duke too
And even though it wasn't in my plans
I tried to raise him the best that I can
They all had to work while they was in school
Because I couldn't afford to give them what they wanted
me too
And I gave each of them a bill that was due
So they could learn some responsibility too
And because they had no male role model
I was as loving as a mother but stern like a father
And even though something came up everyday
God still showed up and made a way
And I told them every day to give God praise
Because he's brought this family a mighty long way

"EVALUATE"

Sometimes I have to evaluate myself
Because I'm no better than anyone else
It's very easy to write a book
Before taking a closer look
And I know it's hard during this walk
Not to gossip when you're having a talk
And even though I've changed from what I used to do
I still find myself gossiping too
So in order not to be seen doing the things I write
I sometimes have to evaluate my life

"REJECTED"

We've all experienced rejection during our life
But mine was from a relationship that didn't turn out right
But if he had rejected me when it begin
It wouldn't have hurt so much when it was about to end
But instead of being honest about what he wanted to do
He went behind my back and did as he choose
And then one day I saw him on a date
And I had my proof but it was a little too late
But I wish he had told me from the start
Instead of rejecting me and breaking my heart
Because the worst thing that a person can do
Is reject someone that's in love with you

"A COMPLETION"

Part of my life has come to a completion
Because things have changed during this season
At first I was bound and couldn't see
But by the grace of God now I'm free
And God has sent a man my way
That's promised to keep a smile on my face
And he's not the type that want's to fight
So abuse will no longer be part of my life
My whole lifestyle has begun to change
Not even my thinking is the same
And you can see a difference in my walk
And you definitely can see it in my talk
And since I don't mind planting a seed
I've been blessed with a gift that'll supply all my needs
And since a completion has taken place
My new life begins today

"STORM"

Most people don't seem to recognize
That a storm is meant to open your eyes
A storm can tear down a happy home
And leave you hurt and all alone
But some storms are worse than others
That's why we should pray for our sisters and brothers
You could have a family member that's living wrong
And a storm could come to see if you're strong
That's why during a storm you should always pray
Because that's the only way to keep satin away
And a storm can make you change your life
From a lifetime of sin to living for Christ
Storms are designed to test what you believe
And devastating enough to knock you to your knees
But the help you need only God can send
So if you withstand the storm you'll be
victorious in the end

"DISTRACTIONS"

The enemy is sending distractions my way
And I'm seeing them vividly every day
Because he knows my books will inspire someone's life
To help them stop sinning and start living right
And now he's sending distractions every day
Hoping that one of them get in my way
But God has given me a ministry to do
And that's to tell the world what I've been through
So it don't matter if it's family or friends
Distractions won't stop the messages that
I'm trying to send

"DREAMS"

I remember when my sister and I was young
Talking to our friends was our way of having fun
We shared our dreams about what we wanted to do
And hoped that one day they'd all come true
We vowed we'd never be hit by a man
Not knowing down the line what was in Gods' plan
Because each of us at some given time
Has experienced physical abuse down the line
But by being abused it caused us to pray
And it made us the women we are today
But it's not too late for our dreams to come true
If we allow God to direct us in everything we do

"MILLIONAIRE"

Ever since I've been blessed with the gift to write
People have been contacting me left and right
Because God has opened up so many doors
So I can be blessed like never before
And I've seen in the spirit the time is here
For me to become a millionaire this year
But first he took me through years of lack
To make sure I wasn't turning back
But when I was ready to establish a name
He knew that I wasn't going to change
And he showed me my blessing had always been there
Because my testimonies is what will make me a
millionaire

"CRYING"

Most people say that crying cleanses the soul
It takes away the hurt from some painful blows
Whether the pain is physical or comes from the heart
After the tears is when the healing can start
The bible says "Weeping may endure for a night
But joy comes in the morning light"
So after you've cried and your wounds begin to mend
That's when God will allow the healing to begin
But healing is a process that takes some time
And it can't begin until you've cleared your mind
It's like being at the funeral of someone close to you
Crying is what helps usher the family through
So don't look at crying as being a weak act
Because Jesus even wept and that's a known fact

"SCARED"

When I'm reading my poetry I know people can see
That I'm not scared when they're looking at me
Because God didn't give me the spirit of fear
But he gave me a boldness to do his will
And whether people will receive it or turn away
I'll still tell about his goodness anyway
Because God has always shed his grace
And he said "don't be scared of men in their faces"
And that's why I can stand and honestly say
That God has brought me a mighty long way
And because I'm not scared I can boldly speak
About the goodness of God and what he's done for me

"DO IT AGAIN"

We all know how the saying ends
Once you do something you'll do it again
And most of my adult life
I've done things I knew wasn't right
But because we do things again and again
Doesn't mean the cycle can't end
Because all things are possible to those who believe
And God proved that by changing me
Because at one time I gambled every day
And God took my addiction away
But that part of my life has come to an end
And even though I did it once I'll never do it again

"THE SPOUSE"

When you're in a marriage and don't appreciate your
spouse
You can eventually push them out the house
And don't say that's' what they wanted to do
Because you played a major role in it too
And now you're crying and putting down his name
When you know in your heart you're part of the blame
Because when he came to you for love & affection
You gave him nothing but total rejection
He even made sure the bills were paid
And you wouldn't even kiss him to start his day
He did everything a spouse could do
But you took it for granted he'd never leave you
And when he realized he couldn't get what he needed
from his spouse
It caused him to go outside the house
And by letting him leave seeking advice
You gave the devil room to let someone in his life
Most people are searching for that special mate
So appreciate what you have before it's too late

"EXPOSED"

In every relationship I've ever been in
I've always had a cheating friend
But what they failed to understand
Is they had my heart in their hand
But no matter what I tried to do
They started arguments out of the blue
And I knew they were doing something on the side
That obviously they were trying to hide
And what they were doing only God knows
But one day it will all be exposed
Because the God we serve sits high and looks low
And eventually all secrets will be exposed

"PRETENDING

When my friend and I met he treated me like a queen
But lately everything he says sound so mean
I know our relationship has started to change
Because the way he use to act is no longer the same
When he's with his friends he'll talk all day
But when we're alone he has nothing to say
And I refuse to pretend like everything's alright
Just to say I have a man in my life
But he won't admit that something is wrong
Even though I keep saying "I'm tired of being alone"
But in the beginning I loved him so much
That every day I longed for his touch
But now I'm noticing that each passing day
I'm seeing myself pushing him away
But I still love this man with all my might
And one day was hoping to become his wife
But I can't continue going through each day
Pretending I'm happy living this way

"ASSIGNMENT"

God has given me an assignment to do
But I'm scared that I won't see it through
I toss and turn all night long
Trying to figure out what I'm doing wrong
He's directed my footsteps in every way
And he also tells me what to say
But writing was only my assignment from the start
To show how much I've humbled my heart
But now I feel at this point in my life
He wants more from me than just to write
And he's placing people in my life that know
How to help my ministry grow
Because the assignment that's been placed on my life
Is to bring others out of darkness and into his
marvelous light

"NATURAL HIGH"

When people find out I don't drink or smoke
They often ask me "What it is I do to cope?"
But I make it a practice to pray each day
And ask God to take these temptations away
Because I want my body to be a sacred place
Where he can dwell and have his way
So when he reveals signs and wonders to me
I can receive the revelation he wants me to see
But praying doesn't only help me get by
It keeps me on a natural high

"A SINGLE MARRIED WOMAN"

Single and married woman are both the same
One is just carrying a man's last name
There's nothing that a single woman can do
That a single married woman couldn't do too
But it's hard for married women to comply with Gods' plan
Because most of them are no longer with their man
And when they meet someone he'll tell them all the time
"As long as you're married you'll never be mine"
And we really want them to fall in love with us
But we're scared they'll betray our love and trust
That's why single married woman will break down and do
Whatever it takes to get you to fall in love too
So don't let a blessing pass you by
If a single married woman catches your eyes

"SIN WITHIN"

It's hard to go through life each day
Trying to do everything the right way
Because no matter what I attempt to do
The sin within won't allow me too
I can have good intentions in my head
But the sin within takes control instead
And I'll start doing things I know is wrong
Because I let my guard down and stop standing strong
But one thing the bible allowed me to see
Was greater is he that resides in me
So I must stand strong, have faith and believe
If I'm planning to overcome the sin within me

"LAST DAY"

If this was the last day I had on earth
I could rest and assure I've proven my worth
Because after everything I've done in my life
I was given a chance to make it right
And now I'm leaving a legacy behind
That could help the world through some trying times
And since it'll be the last day
That I'll be able to see my families face
I'd look into each of their eyes
And plead with them not to cry
Because I don't want my last day on earth
To be filled with sorrow, despair and hurt
Because we all knew the day would come
That this race would be over that we have to run
But if I'm rejoicing on my last day
At least I'll be happy when I pass away

ABOUT THE AUTHOR

Janice Stampley Means was born in Natchez, Mississippi and currently resides in Spartanburg, S.C. She is an active member of the Pentecostal Church under pastorship of Thomas J. Lee.

It is an honor to present the life inspiring words of Janice S. Means. No matter what your religious beliefs, you will find shelter from confusion and sorrow from her undying faith in the healing mercy of God.

Her prose and poetry reflect the voice and tone of the Deep South. These truths of God's love and blessings are gathered from her life experiences and expressed with deep conviction. This book is a present help for all in time of spiritual need.